# Streetwise

David Burridge

Published by Leaf by Leaf
an imprint of Cinnamon Press
www.cinnamonpress.com

The right of David Burridge to be identified as author of this work has been asserted by him in accordance with the Copyright, Designs and Patent Act, 1988. © 2021, David Burridge.
ISBN 978-1-78864-926-1

British Library Cataloguing in Publication Data. A CIP record for this book can be obtained from the British Library.

All rights reserved. No part of this publication may be reproduced, stored in a retrieval system, or transmitted in any form or by any means, electronic, mechanical, photocopying, recording or otherwise without the prior written permission of the publishers. This book may not be lent, hired out, resold or otherwise disposed of by way of trade in any form of binding or cover other than that in which it is published, without the prior consent of the publishers.

Designed and typeset in Bodoni by Cinnamon Press.
Cover design by Adam Craig © Adam Craig from original artwork:
201403543 © Tiff20 | Dreamstime.com
Cinnamon Press is represented by Inpress.

## Acknowledgements

I would like to thank all the people who gave me inspiration to write these poems and to explore humanitarian values through my poetry.

My involvement with the *Backroom Poets* has enabled me to develop my style over the years, and a while ago I was fortunate to receive valuable coaching from the poet and mentor, Elaine Baker.

Last but not least, I am grateful to my wife, Helga Markert, for her initial editing and structuring these poems into a collection for submission.

# Contents

## Encounters in the Street

| | |
|---|---|
| Outside Broadcasts | 11 |
| Beats Like Blakey | 12 |
| Morning Progress | 13 |
| Giving Old George a Hand | 14 |
| Outing | 15 |
| Sworn In | 16 |
| The English Tourist | 17 |
| Unsettled | 18 |
| Small Change | 19 |
| White Van Driver | 20 |
| On a Winter's Afternoon | 21 |
| Reflections of a Street Cleaner | 22 |
| An Evangelist | 23 |
| At Your Service | 24 |
| Hitch-hiker | 25 |
| When the Bell Rang | 26 |
| Off the Map | 27 |
| Juxtaposed | 28 |
| On the Edgware Road. | 29 |
| Climbing Up Richmond Hill | 30 |
| Falling off Canary Wharf | 31 |
| Underfoot in Cologne | 32 |

## Then and Now

| | |
|---|---|
| Berlin Encounters | 35 |
| Welcome to the Forum Willy Brandt! | 36 |
| Geneva Conventions | 37 |
| Praha | 38 |
| Asylum Seeker | 39 |
| Hans Litten | 40 |
| Stone Silence | 41 |
| From Names to Numbers | 42 |
| Strawberry Girl | 43 |
| Elbow Grease | 44 |
| An Aunt Sometimes Visited | 45 |
| Last Frame | 46 |

## Paths Taken

| | |
|---|---|
| A Simple Gait | 49 |
| The Folly | 50 |
| Bohinj Recalled | 51 |
| Sweet Chestnuts in the Cevennes | 52 |
| Place De La Fontaine | 53 |
| Caves of Perigord | 54 |
| Bonjour Madame! | 55 |
| Along the Canal Du Midi | 56 |
| Tripping Up Montsegur | 57 |

## In Waiting

| | |
|---|---|
| Head And Neck | 61 |
| Keeping An Appointment | 62 |
| Why Me? | 63 |
| Inoperable | 64 |
| Sharing | 65 |
| Service User | 66 |
| Left Behind | 67 |
| Clearing Out | 68 |

## Down and Out

| | |
|---|---|
| Hot Desking | 71 |
| A Few Words Before Leaving | 72 |
| Down and Out | 73 |
| On a Point of Leaving | 74 |
| Short-listed | 75 |
| Journey's End | 76 |
| The Last Brown Packet | 77 |
| Workaholic | 78 |
| Derelict Factory | 79 |

| | |
|---|---|
| Notes on Poems | 81 |

# Streetwise

# Encounters in the Street

## Outside Broadcasts

I study-stare within a second's split,
catching not so much full-face
but edges and angles,
strain or sweep of smiles,
not at me of course. For I am like glass,
a prism, through which stories refract:

>street musician concertos with city noise
>his cadenza unheard
>but behind his begging hat
>he winks for a coin-toss
>
>strapped into her wheelchair, she trains her withered torso
>to catch his tune
>hardly a snatch, then she is rolled on
>eyes angled to something up there
>something out of sight
>
>the high-scaffolding shout won't be clearly heard
>but a picture of rants is caught by bottom-step eyes
>fluent in bolts and girder talk
>
>tethered-together tourists broad-sweep the pavement
>kerbing resistance
>staring at historic stone
>never disconnecting even at close quarters
>
>young mother steers her bustling unit
>half on wheels, half skipping to the rhythm of pavement cracks
>orders *hurry*
>choking on a sly puff
>
>along a pavement passage
>the old man's dog strains an angle towards
>as if there's more to say
>but he's lead-snagged to a straight ahead
>though he'll lean again tomorrow

# Beats Like Blakey

*Beggar in Birmingham*

Lidless paint-bins upended percussion.
He rolls on his kit to catch a donation.
Pavement solo needs to stretch – no ensemble
to swing with him on this New Street gig.

Wristing his sticks to commuter steps, he gives them
down-beat to stamp home to, tempo to finger click.
But his plastic rhythm is wasted in the random shuffle;
they all pass without a clink.

Shops are shuttered, crowding fizzles,
he crashes cymbals in his head.

Then up from stone a bass line strums,
out of a dark-door a blues horn moans,
headlight flash shines a trumpet.
All tethered to his tight rhythm brushwork,
they swing together for his final riff.

# Morning Progress

He slams the warped door in the spasm of a curse,
locking his own bent bones into place.
She fumbles for his hand instead of a stick,
a reminder of the time when their hand-hold was
a continuation of what went on inside.

Just as hard shafts dazzle at window height,
they proceed, canvass bag gripping as if it might resist
the expedition, as they like to call it, to buy
this and that, stretch the day's purpose and
scatter smiles at strangers they ought to know.

Earlier they had spilt some temper, like a last dab of
expensive perfume. This frail snap barely echoed
their young fights, when the whole world had to be cited.
Something old had been smashed, it had tumbled
from a dithered grab. Their dentures bit fume until
it slipped away; they were at least still standing.

Steady-stepping, awkward-grasping, they progress
commenting on any slight shift of things,
avoiding the polystyrene splat of some
over-nourished drunk. Soon fingers of warm sun
touch their faces and they silently agree
to pass the day together after all.

# Giving Old George a Hand

Gulped at the lean of the breeze-waved ladder,
which he climbed with ease above my earth-rooted fears.
We began our climb to the sagging gutter,
fixed workman's botch or gusted smash.

His were ballet steps sprinting on high slates,
with a posture to make a super-model swoon.
I was skin-scratched, wobble-footed, knee-creased,
stuck to the roof-slope just like a snail.

Heading up stone-crush, rung by rung,
neck veins livid, soft hat cushioning the sting.
I rub-killed moss stain, dangling acid tin
ignoring devil thoughts of upside down.

Down from the roof we trucked to beer break,
griping about boss above the cabin din.
Over road bumps we shared our wished-for;
he had promises long forgotten,
I had visions beyond the pale.

Back with George on our high roof work,
until cold winds ballooned my shirt.
I knew it was time to go to earth.
Left him up high sure-footing his loadbearing,
until the day he air-stepped an end.

## Outing

Blank walls crowd him, the tap drips a slow march,
so he unrumples his old suit, slips on his
more scraped than polished black shoes.
Slams his warped door in spasm of a curse, then
sets off into town, at a remembered business pace.

A welcome swamp of noise lifts his face,
there are eyes to be met, nods to be occasioned,
and if he could harvest a few smiles to glow later
in remembered scraps, that would be a special treat.

Crossing the road is not recommended; black-tinted
road-snarlers have sworn never to give way.
Traffic lights pulsate a few seconds' dash.
Why risk the nothing he has, in a pointless rush?

He mumbles at Malls that scour your credit,
bundle you out with too much – *best before trash*.
Recalls trading over teak counters,
goods wrapped for rung-up cash.
His dangling bag is now a rarely filled sack, except
for bruised fruit found round the back.

He slows to a dodge, edging pavement huddles,
The scrums stay tight until loosened by selfies.
Arm-sweeps from posers totter him to the edge.
Time for him to return to his album of snaps.

# Sworn In

Picked off the street, out of a hat,
called in to consider cold facts.
None from outside, just what is here:
pink-ribboned bundle, witness mumble,
or through security-glass stare.

Barristers grin me through argument.
I am wig-scratched through questions.
They gown-tug toward submissions.
I am a pal – for now. Judge
reads me a story – just written;
a box of logic for me to step into.

Unreasonable doubt worms my
sense – I find it inside dangling
like a gas mask, still in its wrapper.
I finger-fold a hard headline
but don't want to jump to its taint,
echoing someone else's take.

Time to weigh up, wear the blindfold.
Locked in until we decide,
and then the bell rings:
Is he guilty, or am I?

# The English Tourist

She lolls in unexpected Richmond heat,
designer holes in her sleeves,
tan topping-up selected spots.
Easing in this café spill,
she holds forth; tight-gripping,
frog-marching the theme.

It was her French holiday,
no time-share tampering for her,
she possessed all that it contained.
The whole French nation captured,
for ten days half-board, without
laying one beach towel down.

The breakfast must be her treat,
for I see no tethers on her listeners' seats.
Her volume and pitch carefully adjusted,
so new entrants can be easily admitted.
If eye contact wanders unsupervised,
she effects an immediate *Anschluss*
into her circle of smiles and sighs.

Sighing with completed pleasure,
she releases her clutch on the conversation,
allowing escape to other table-wobbles.
Still she has been careful not to reveal.
spots where the tan has begun to peel.

# Unsettled

I recall *pea-soupers* made us stay behind walls,
bordered by the creep of fog,
we kept fire crouching, flame staring,
listening to tales of trench-coated stranglers
slipping by in the wet waft outside,
until the border lifted beyond the grey slate,
and all was deemed safe – though dark
shivers always lingered.

Jammed in a carriage steel-tracking,
across mist-smothered fields, I crouch
in a soft seat, dirty window staring. Near to me,
amid penned and jostled, a loud voice declares:
*Reminds me of pea-souper years, we all looked out
for each other then, not like now!* I listened in disbelief,
felt old scares returning.

# Small Change

It was not so bad really, looking back -
a corridor life with a door bang at the end.
Of course they didn't dare dream beyond
a grub of garden manured by the milk-man's horse.
Clean lace curtains, for the curler-headed Missus
to ward off the world.

He hunched to the office in his seat-crumpled suit,
blew dust from the files he once copper-plated;
logged every item never needed from the store.

Sundays, they droned liturgy hoping for a warming,
a spark in the corner, for the avoidance of doubt.
Later nibbled beef lunch, then locked the bedroom door.

The *sit up and beg* rarely left the kerb. Perhaps
part of an escape plan, but they always returned
from Clacton-shingles braced for another year.

Later when the coal-scuttle became a burden,
they bought synthetic, sealed with bright Formica.
A nice young man did it without a fuss; quick in and out
so as not disturb the dust.

Gas fire warmed them until monoxide slipped them on;
if to a parallel world, then it was just the next door along.

# White Van Driver

Appearing inked to his elbows,
old tattoos smudged but not removed;
items of identity remain like some stubborn dream.
He leans a spit from the frame of his wound-down,
then head in his hand, he snarls at the red lights.
Will they ever let him *go like the clappers*?
At last it's green but the column just creeps.
He revs and grinds his anger.
What does he have in his blank van that is so urgent?
Nothing to be advertised or left on your doorstep. Suddenly
he is off and away, leaving us to choke on his diesel smoke.

## On a Winter's Afternoon

Sour light thickens and dims – unspoken curfew prevails.
But you shirt-sleeve the gauntlet of cold gusts,
to jam inside the pub-door swing and
shout; *Its cold!* – A secret worth sharing?
Later, warm-headed, you'll brazen it home,
daring pneumonia to lay you down.

Amid the pack now, some lean as if to whisper.
Instead spit out loud-talk on this and that,
noise mingling like unchecked smoke.

Others crouch in corners, they grimace
over lined-up glasses. A few gulps then,
time to pick up tasks and tools of usual living.

You spill loud thoughts, dodging interruptions
Holding on to your *telling point* – nobody is listening.
They laugh at a punch-line you didn't deliver -
your shout frames their own ideas. In turn you elbow
edge-way entries with topic changes.
Now time is called and the din is swilled-back.
So we all go out into the frozen black.

## Reflections of a Street Cleaner

Winter dawn still not cracked:
    *Someone forgot to pay the gas.*
A fluorescent trundle, pausing, picking,
Pavement bruised with last night's sick.
Hand crushed cans, big-deal meal half-bitten;
    *Diners lifted into space for a closer look.*

Each item pincer-lifted, arm's length for hygiene:
    *Precious objects for an installation.*
    *I'd call it: Binned Shit.*
 Handcart rolls on to the next bits.
    *All spick and span for heals' nine o'clock click*

Corners scraped and brushed:
    *Dirt rearranged for mid-morning choke.*
At one angle of bricks,
    *Where sweet wrappers usually slink*
Bright eyes pierce the gloom,
    *Sharper than my hi-vis vest*
Feathers arranged to hide the bleeding;
    *Don't remember this on my NVQ list.*
Head twisted, beak tries to peck.
    *What's the use of going without a fight?*

Dawn bleeds, his cheek glistens,
    *Another fucking shift done and dusted.*

# An Evangelist

Rasping at the footfall passing his pulpit kerb,
hoarse before a single sinner is saved.
Choking on out- of- town dust, they are
within spitting distance of his gospel shout.

But they only see the glass-cased call:
*Today is your last chance, closing down sale,*
*everything must go.*

A congregation queues at the cash point,
His crumpled flyers tumble the news:
*Everlasting torment, avoid it today!*
But two for the price of one is heaven sent.
Their promised land, just a bag-swing away.

This land was once a gentle heath,
until the diggers ground down nature.
The crooked has been straightened,
rough places made plain.
Now in this squared-off paved wilderness,
a prophet's message is in vain.

I could join him, to shake the dry land,
break up the stones and let the green return.
But next Saturday where would he offer salvation?
Where would they throng to finger their dreams?

Perhaps it's me walking in the darkness
and they who have seen a great light.

## At Your Service

Cross the threshold – he smiles you in.
Space is stretched in his dingy-wall squeeze.
You edge the chair like a condemned man,
he pushes your seat firmly home.

The table wobbles a thimble-vase,
its single rose droops in your direction.
With a flick of his wrist, the napkin display
is deflowered. The menu is background reading.
You may pick a chalked-up special,
then neatly sip time until he deems it due.

Blinded by a dish of steam, you gesticulate praise,
then sleeve the bread basket onto the floor,
panic like an altar boy who has dropped the host,
hoping they are still wafers when they hit the ground.

*Is everything to your taste?*

Don't be tempted to complain. Best to
avoid the cold march with your plate,
the Chef's sorrows, wrung out of him,
behind the swing doors. Just swallow
the chokes and cough up a smile.

The waiter angles and turns between the tables
He'll eventually let you catch his eye,
terrorises you with his keypad.
Just punch in your gratitude.
It's your only way out.

# Hitch-hiker

Been abandoned; got to get to Taunton.
Don't go out of your way.
Just a bit of a journey. Soon be home.
That's the great thing!

Looks like trouble ahead, snarling sky.
Got a lift just in time.
Just drop me anywhere.
I'll know where I am when I get there.
That's the great thing!

Got a daughter, lives close by.
She's waiting for me!
Can't remember the address,
I'll know it when I see it.
That's the great thing!

I used to be a bank manager hereabouts.
Knew this road like the back of my hand.
But all the trees have grown.
It's an area I don't think I know.

Had a Golf like that.
Wanted to change it for something bigger.
Can't remember where I am parked.
Just dumped really.

Are we going North or South?
Don't put yourself out.
Drop me anywhere.
That's the great thing!
Taunton you say?
I used to live quite near there.

## When the Bell Rang

I downed my twist of stairs to let in the world:
Parcel, a poster or something to be read.

Two ladies smiled my polite attention, with
A Universal Being to be found in a book.

Their faith rested in perfect translation -
They poked at their I-pads for prophetic proof.

I traded doubts and fingered their proof,
Heard myself say: *Question everything -*

*That way you'll be elevated beyond the self.*
We all wanted to rattle the status-quo.

But instead door stepped a perfect end:
Them in heaven and me just below.

# Off the Map

*Lost in the London Borough of Stratford*

Smudge on the page of my spine-broke city guide,
puzzles me along the high street for a turning,
an alley with a name but no stretch. Steel fences
have rounded up the land for Olympic glory.
High risers bully the scene with their layered misery,
at ground level, the cold anger of stale graffiti.

Back along the lane, once lined-up Victorian well-to-dos,
now host front parlour churches and dream-snapping stores.
They buy gold or sell you tarnish, offering the unloaded ,
a phone crackle home, polyphony of poor voices.
Cheques cashed for the minimum wage they never saw.
Scrimped dosh, free market for the underhanded.

Mid-morning street scratched by a low light.
The long limbed lady has finished her night shift,
draws on a fag through tight-knit fingers,
appointments made on a mobile phone.

A saunter of youths consider attendance,
put it to a voice vote, then rush to something cool.
Here is a scurry of kids, black faces still shining,
trying not to be lined up by the hip-swaying matron,
who sing-soothes and flocks them into school.

Town hall cleaned to impress craning necks, but
nobody looks up to the Italianate arches.
The chambers below echo with clicking heels
and somebody whistling.

At the end of the high road there is a church with a tree.
A squinting eye might conjure up a village green
like it was, before tarmac rolled out prosperity.

# Juxtaposed

*Somewhere in South London*

Not really neighbours; just abutting,
Distance secured with wrought iron crafting,
lets light or a curious finger poke through
to ignite a snarl and a uniformed shout.

On this side: sixties' slap-dash fitted with gaps, cracks
and softwood rot, grassy verges bloomed with litter.
Someone's knickers, clothes line dangled,
without the will to flutter.

Through high gates, measured scan, beyond heavy shoulders,
licensed to block, arched stone, shines like laundered gold.
Buildings pomped with age, blot out their shivering surrounds
with rampant Rhododendron swathe.

*JUST SUPPOSE* –

Iron melted and stone crumbled, *neighbours* came suddenly face to face.
Would hard cash and body-hurt quickly change hands; perhaps
a great passing-by on the other side, or would they wonder,
how sight and smell could so divide members of the same tribe?

## On the Edgware Road.

An afternoon of winter sunshine,
business spills from café doors.
Balding men flute sour coffee,
exploring closure of handshake deals.

Hands spell out arguments.
I see beads counted, then abandoned.
The debate is taut, about to snap,
loosens again to a lean-back chat.

Young men sit in contemplation.
Hookah pipes bubble beside them,
their apparatus wobbling
over pavement cracks.

Fruit and veg is boastfully piled.
Ripeness to be touched and tested.
Burka-smothered ladies barter
with their naked eyes.

A beggar wanders through the crowds,
plying her trade in rhythmic pleadings,
she carries a baby that never ages.

Flimsy sheets of news are fingered.
Readers know they are out of date.
Real news comes through the family,
Street corner whispers, mobile links.

A fragment of Beirut has seeded here
on this high London road.
Exotic fragments drifting on the wind,
vanish into Edwardian stone.

# Climbing Up Richmond Hill

Pink joggers beside me, skipping on the balls of their feet,
wired to a certain song, they hint a smile,
or perhaps it's early orders chanted in their heads,
app-prepping for another day in the open plan.

My knees are steeled for a panting stumble.
I stare at the configured stone, changing
style with each house passed, as if there had been
an architectural spat across the centuries. Each outcome
worth more than I have ever owned.

Soon my gaze slips down to a spread of Thames.
Used to its gentle Oxfordshire winding, here
it seems to swell up for a capital flood.

These soft hills ease the eyes,
while heavy business drones below.
But now a squirrel stops in front –
I expect a quick blink, then a swift scurry up a safe branch.
No! Market forces have nurtured him to shift close.
His eye turns a question on me: *where are they then?*

## Falling off Canary Wharf

Market glitches – he considers a leap from the high window,
splashed with evening gold – has seen it done in old
black and white, but Health and Safety sealed the frame.
The only smooth journey down from this trading tower,
a lift solemnly stating each lowering for posterity.

On the ground, almost intact, identity frozen on a tenth floor screen,
glass door slides him out, bars him coming back again.

Throbbing squares have thinned out to isolation; usual haunts
are body-packed. He has no wish to writhe or crush.
Half-eaten snacks bob on wharf-water
green slime; he thinks only silk shirt stains.
So he steps away into the old Poplar streets.

## Underfoot in Cologne

I foot-slip, recover, and look down.
Five squint-small plaques embedded but proud.
Members of the same family bully-pushed through
their own front door, into a blind van.
Lugging cases, hardly filled, yet more than they would need.
It's seventy years or so,
their house long since swallowed by marble walls,
their trail now a stretch of city rush.

I trip to meet tomb-less names and whisper-wish;
perhaps one survived, sat old in the park, in a wince of sun.
There must be other plaques across this city – in other
cities – other countries. Every cold victim should be
so honoured, until pavements strain under the weight
of brass, and we all stumble, never to forget.

But what about Gaza?
Where city lives are muscled in by military might.
Young people can only look down and see the broken stone,
from so many years before.

# Then and Now

# Berlin Encounters

I expected to be dwarfed by history in high stone,
angles and arches constructed by this and that power.
A whole industry of remembrance, from bits of the wall
to dark Holocaust blocks. We stumbled up *Berliner Dom*,
not to look up at heaven, but down to city seethe.
Then through *Brandenburger Tor* – of course who wouldn't?
*Charlottenburg* was empty to my eye.
It was the comfortable avenues that somehow settled me,
and the soft green surrounds of the *Tiergarten*.
We made our way along the *Landwehrkanal* bank,
at a steady pace to the chorus of caged animals.
Suddenly I was quietly faced with stone letters angled,
as if about to be tossed into waste water.
*Rosa Luxemburg* – a remembered disposal;
I felt a sharp bite of history at this site.

# Welcome to the Forum Willy Brandt!

History student toured us past Willy's episodes,
carefully encased. Scenes acted before she was born,
brought back, freshened up, dusted down.
His perfect kneel in Warsaw gave us all a quiet gulp.
We paused to discuss a time when beliefs could be
lifted shoulder high; the future then was a function of hope.
We came to the end, our guide slipped away, she had
exams to complete, a world to find sense in.

# Geneva Conventions

*In the Old Town*

Above the swarm of designer labels and expensive scents,
we knee-twist along the steep streets, under old buildings
that lean together to shadow out the sunlight, but keep the tourists in.
Finally resting in Café Socrates – *what's your poison?* I am invited.
I mumble Calvin, and a beer bottle appears.
His labelled face grims me a stare.
I toast his once good health. Then consider is it all predetermined?
I'll just wait and see.

*Allée Des Nations*

An industry of missions tidied behind lines of quiet trees.
Global issues are wrangled by groups of joggers sweating
through their lunch breaks. Selfie-sticks are raised to
capture each "me" before the line of patterned flapping,
scattering triviality far and wide.
An old African man sits on a bench, crouched over, his hand
smothering his quiet survivor tears.
In the distance, Mont Blanc white-snows me a sneer:
*Why aren't you here?*

*Broken Chair*
Monument in Geneva by Swiss artist Daniel Berset constructed by Louis Genève

As high as a house, but framed for a kitchen,
discomforting seat stands firm with its broken leg.
I stare at the stump and notice – not severed nor chopped,
nor rotted away, but built to last to remind us all,
how many limbs have been torn from their sockets,
how many limbless will never sit up straight again.

# Praha

*Skyline*

Gold boils up with each high glance.
Thousands of elegant windows rim the streets,
studded with churches in a squabble of style.
Gothic or Baroque all just high pokes of stone,
taking their turn to call the tune.
But beneath? How many stumbles have there been?
How much blood has seeped these cobbles?

*Swarming on Charles Bridge*

Every object crafted to sparkle, then trellis-piled
to stay the horde of bulging limbs; the stride of shorts.
Multitudes of musicians play trimmed-off well-knowns.
Deep among the standing-by, a man crouches under sack-cloth,
playing his part in the trickle-down. I thought-finger a coin-toss.

*Statues on Stairs*
*Memorial to victims of communism*

Each step up breaks off a piece of man, until just unstumbled legs remain.
Trip down and he is back together – fit to stagger on again.
Somewhere outside, in a quiet corner I see it granite framed:
*a working-man*; capped and hunched for toil.
Is he straight and tall now, trading his talents or left leaning over a bin?

# Asylum Seeker

I am the face out of place in your supermarket aisles.
Forgive me if I stare at your high-stacked shelves,
I used to queue for the last stale scrap. Now I swing
my bag with a small white sliced inside.

I tap through your cold streets, wait in the gutter,
to catch your coin-tossed kindness,
at arm's length for my callipered legs,
though I know I disturb you like upswept litter.

My identity is a tatter, thinned by official fingering.
My flash-startled face fading and creased.
It's the smudge on the date that keeps me safe,
until the day my dossier is found.

Your mumble locks me out, you speak like a rattling train.
When I have learnt enough to decouple your vowels,
parry the stab of your consonant sounds,
I will find out what lies behind that English smile.

You ask me, *Don't you ever think of going home?*
I am always there, it's a warm kitchen in my head.
But my thoughts are splintered and memories rubble,
and the people I talk to are dead.

# Hans Litten

*The man who took Hitler to court*

You stumbled him with a sweet sting of questions;
answers you already knew. His sprawl was your end.
You could have flown, but your Golgotha gene
stayed you to defend the abused.
Human rights enacted, not lifeless on a page.

Pulped towards death, Rilke's rhythms
still danced in your head.
You sang your final song, *Die Gedanken sind frei*.
Before you choked the pain.

Anger still catches when we see old footage,
brown sleeves grasp armfuls of books;
reason and humanity tossed to the flames.
Scenes that sew yellow stars in all of us.

## Stone Silence

Your head bent away from any check-up stare.
Alone in a queue is better than a gallow's walk.
Just the clutch of a *Persilschein*, then on-board.

What of your suitcase soul, packed with the past?
Incidents strapped tight in the dark. For each
memory released might lodge a claim.

And what of nights when dreams
claw through, old screams unmuffle,
and waking's like a trap-door rattle? Still better
you say than hard staring at stone walls.

Of course there were stories that grazed the truth.
Corners turned to somewhere loud and lived-in.
But once in a while the secrets will snatch away smiles
and steer you back to what is petrified.

# From Names to Numbers

*Pictures in Sachsenhausen Museum in Oranienburg*

A queue all hatted and wrapped-up,
some even with trench coats.
Perhaps yellow stars were sewn
underneath and out of sight.
Leather bags tightly grasped,
containing needs quickly reached for.
They lean towards each other,
frowning at whispered explanations.

It's eighty-one years since they stood there,
that entry to *Sachsenhausen*.
The lucky ones became migrants,
travelling along tracks and roads,
carrying their names to some dreamt freedom,
just like those now found bobbing on the sea.

Others went through the gate,
beyond the sign: *Arbeit macht frei*.
Their names to be replaced with tattooed numbers,
adding to the final count.
Every name must be remembered.

# Strawberry Girl

A startle out of shuttered night,
she stood in Reception with a joyous shout;
she had crossed the killing line.

*Vopos* busy shredding their past;
no change of mind was all she hoped for,
sprinting through the empty checkpoint.

She was patted and clapped, led to top of the table.
Carte Blanche offered, but the kitchen was shut.
So a stack of strawberries was placed before her,
fit for party boss without the need to queue.

Her eyes grew like reflected moons.
Eat up they said, your dash to freedom
is in season; over there will soon be here.
Her story dribbled out amid the mouthfuls,
face shining with juice and tears.

A slip of years; the Trabant stink is now antique,
Beethoven is no longer sobbed, scrambling
has replaced queuing, but grabbing still done
by the pallet load.

A chambermaid in a small hotel, stripping
a soiled bed tries to recall strawberries
she once tasted – stacked so high.

# Elbow Grease

Mum skivvied for couch clinicians in ample villas
off the Finchley Road.
Attics cluttered, cellars locked,
windows staring at high garden walls.

She straightened out their creases,
leaked light through heavy velvet,
polished floors to leg-break shine,
ordered their books to stand upright.

On the way out she let neurosis in;
well-heeled martyrs to polite repression.
They skulked passed her terrifying mop
for an hour of supine dismantling.

The kitchen was her consulting room
where the good doctors begged for their coffee,
craving to talk about the lines they crossed.
She always had an ear for them, albeit a little deaf.

Those heavy duty thinkers untied the psychic knots.
Spills were left for Mum to clear.
Some stains are stubborn, *Never mind*, she'd say,
*hard scrubbing staunches tears.*

Once she soft-trod up the stairs, with a steadied teacup.
The doctor she dusted for, clinically couching his only leg,
quietly told her: In Auschwitz he lost his soul. Friends gassed,
but he survived, though they still called to him in his head.

He bit pills when she went out, was dead when she next went in
A big room was no terrifying void for her,
another floor to polish was space to dream.
Salvation earned through elbow grease, paradise found in a gleam.

Too weak to wipe away the piling dust,
when she finally lay amid her own clutter.

# An Aunt Sometimes Visited

Through her door, into a coffee waft.
There's warm cake to loosen my tongue,
though I only have flat stories to tell.

Her plump person hovers to be hugged
in the narrow aisle between the tabled clutter
and the settee that swallows me up.

Heavy wood furniture roots her to the spot
where her young years were polished away,
and memories piled dust-high.

Deep in our séance, she brings the old days,
talks of a time when the pain was fresh,
faces picked out from their sepia graves.

Big-boned men in uniforms are recalled;
how they were before booze burnt them,
their high-spirited ladies, until they sagged.

She dredges up the unforgiving wall.
Remembers the strong hands that built it so high.
Too frail to scale it, they won't meet now before they die.

The resolute clock has turned the afternoon over,
and I have deadlines to meet. She shows she knows
with an at-the-door hug, packing my pocket with journey-grub.

## Last Frame

*Dedicated to the heroism of the German student Sophie Scholl who in 1944 handed out leaflets to students in Munich university criticising the Nazis. She and her brother were executed.*

I first found you in a battered book; one in a rubble of paperbacks, its pencilled price smudged.

Your sacrifice was a footnote; not front page stuff. I was not long out of war comics, firm in the belief that everything was resolved in the last frame.

I have to read myself into those scenes, imagining the unthinkable. I know I have to make that grisly march again; sink to my knees for your sake; follow you to the blade. You chose crucifixion – a last smoke your sour wine. Was defiance a sufficient reward? I cry out now in my dreams: A hideout somewhere must have been possible! *Im Keller,* until the bombing had stopped.

I squander my flabby freedom – yours by rights. They should have let you grow old. You could have found forgiveness in old men's stumble.

I cry out now from the dark night of my soul and try to give the answer to the question that shudders me still. What would I have done?

# Paths Taken

# A Simple Gait

*Reveries of a Solitary Walker by Rousseau*

Somewhere along this forest path,
I stretch my legs in steady steps.
My pace, a breathing space to calm me.
Though here and there a stumble, I am released,
for a while from the clutch of pain,
or even suffocating pleasure.

I can stop and lean against rock or trunk,
or sit on the ground to consider nature,
blooming, swelling, finally a withered flake.
This is the shape my consciousness takes.
A stretch further perhaps I'll see a sunset.
When? – I don't need to know.

The past is a sudden swarm of thoughts.
Like insects, hovering, dipping and stinging,
delivering itches and swellings, though
as with all nature they seer, then all fade,
leaving me to continue my steady pace.

# The Folly

*A hill in Oxfordshire*

Up the slight hill, perched above everything here-about;
a chance to strain eyes, arm-stretch to points wide below.

In winter, we edge along a remembered path,
hearing the snap of bone in each crush of frosted grass.
Above us crows rabble the blank sky.

Circling the crown, one side we are cupped in stillness,
wind-howl ambushed on the other.

Spring is opening time. The ground, though foot-soft,
still allows an easy stride. There is a poke of sudden green,
a smile on the tree-line's frown.

Ice-air thaws to living scent. Rabbits scurry, stall,
vanish back to basement duties.

A bush fidgets, then a whole squabble of song
rising and swooping, bold-brassing as if all is to be owned.

In summer's long light, the *Ridgeway* leans closer,
conspiring to smother the moaning road below.

Butterflies pirouette on petals, wings folded
like praying hands, while boozing bees
grizzle their defiance of gravity. Leaf and blade
open-face to the sloping stroke of sun.

Owners are barked up the hill – reminded
between I-Phone fixes to lever-toss the ball
in some direction to allow leap and bite
before slobbering back home.

In the heat, parents picnic-spread choice litter,
their edgy kids bench-huddle to buckle cans
and float crisp bags, even bounce on wheels.

Autumn leaks from overhead, path becomes a mottled smear.
Far off, amid the stowed-together green, copper burnish
Appears, staging a beautiful end.

# Bohinj Recalled

*A large glacial lake in Slovenia*

On *Triglav*, high above Bohinj's summer heat,
we thrust our fingers into melting snow,
knowing we could descend to warm hands again.
Wondered, just beyond those peaks,
how many frozen arms were laid out
in broken earth?

Down again and skirted the lake,
hard-staring our new acquaintance.
At high noon it was an empty mouth,
swallowing up the whole blue sky,
busy banks ignored the crime.

Trout in brackish huddle, flicked their tails
in irritated unison, yearned to be in the fast flow,
snap at the fly with its steel sting.

Dog promiscuous with his obedience,
trotted with us to the next village,
then vanished into an open door,
without us able to call his name.

Cygnet stuck in a sluice gate;
flurry of international sticks urged it out,
incredulous, its mother didn't beak it free.

Old ladies worked their neat vegetable rows,
until the sun was hard and high.
Then time to be seated under a tree,
and in the gentle shade tear-dab the past.

Evening mountains tossed shadows down.
A dance was screened with the splintered sun.
Locked up church-bells,
peeled from their cover in the hills.
Night-time quietly folded away
all the visions we now recall.

# Sweet Chestnuts in the Cevennes

Now is the time for the fruit to tumble,
as old bones sway in autumn gusts.
Hard ground tickled with canopy shrivel,
Wind-stripped limbs, piteous nudes,
surrounded by a conifer brood.

Crowned leaves in the summer breeze,
velvet sparkle in a sunlight squint; seemed
soft to touch beyond my reach, but
below the bole, thistle-sharp, marshalled
to pierce my careless grasp.

Once this was a Huguenot harvest,
picked and roasted with savoir-faire,
spiked feet danced to split the pods.
Flavour for the plain-word preachers,
gold to nourish their insurrection.

These hills have long since emptied,
no one left to bear the fruit. Just
wind-creak harvest works the scatter.
So casual hooves might split the pods
and bury the seeds in winter rot.

## Place De La Fontaine

Silver flumed from fashioned stone,
then basined back to leaden soak.
I sat amid the tourist-spill and ordered
water to drown my wine.
No twist of cap or popping cork, just
an arm-stretch to brim my glass.

Spill, stretch, brim – acts of laissez-faire
freeze-framed in my head. I hill-tumbled home,
determined to bring hard-graft to an end.

Five years since that first sweat and stumble;
Slow knee bending up sun-stroked slopes,
tripping roots and slipping stones, until sheltered
by a crowd of roofs, kind shadows for the seared.

Today the square sulks in shade, no table clutter.
Café closed – door notice-sealed,
fountain shrunk to a utility. I see for the first time
a metal sign: *non potable*, of course.

# Caves of Perigord

Midst a bee-hum, when the heat was thick
and the sky barefaced, we sand-crackled the path,
sensing something burnt. Too much tanning, but
a decent plane tree arm would shortly shade us.

Curving passed, we missed the dark gapes,
for fresh spring had smothered the story,
and we trekked on, declaring it to be
close to paradise.

Two hundred heretics, cave-hidden,
smoked to death like charcoal burning,
such a careful skill hereabouts – back then.

Field-sweated, bible-gripped, hid in the cool
to read in their *own words*. A heresy beyond belief;
when entrance through the needle's eye
was deemed the vicar's gift.

# Bonjour Madame!

She window-leans out from her living quarters,
a crevice of cottage under the wall.
Puycelsi – a village high above the Forêt de Grésigne,
built to scour and beat off thugs marauding below.
For centuries quiet was contained with height and stone.

In the mid-morning bask, she presents her proud pots,
and while the cat sleeks by, describes the season's blooming.
Her simple sense of completion dosed me with the need
to peel back particulars of a simple day to find the universal,
and this before darkness quietly closes in.

## Along the Canal Du Midi

Stretched ahead, an endless view of soft float.
Curves of calm occasionally carved apart
by yacht-engined piles of over-spiced bellies.
But warm silence would always lap back again.
A tow-path stride would bring us to an ocean,
through green-freckled tunnels; or so we thought.

We strode, cheering Napoleon for his plane tree plant.
Behind us a sting of cycle bells,
a peloton of wasp-headed Lycra stormed past.
The air hung with question marks.
Isn't walking for the poor and defeated?
But we recovered our pace
to a rising weave of birdsong.

Sentries of trees lined our stare through perfect arches.
Then we noticed some shrivel on mottled masts,
painted yellow crosses warned of execution.
Soon the avenue vanished into a stump line,
hot crackle slid our boots.
Squinting in the mad-dog sun,
we saw our dream was at an end.

# Tripping Up Montsegur

This path doesn't welcome me,
wishes me away, binding itself ever tighter
to its siege terrain.

Since its fall, thousands of feet have worn
its stones marble-smooth.

First the Cathars who raised this fortress
to touch the cheek of Heaven.

Steel-clad crusaders bent on holy stabbing.
Later hand-sown leather; erudite bone kickers,
clue-scratching the broken battlements.

Now designer trainers under uncertain knees,
committed to getting our Euros' worth.
Chance to breath-take at the postcard top.

Listen! Beyond our panting and pumping,
there is another footfall still to be heard,
folded into the moaning wind.

The quick steps of heretics running to their *Endure*,
in the car park below, absolving each other and dancing to the flames,
beating the Catholics at their own game.
My tired feet cannot comprehend their surefootedness.

# In Waiting

# Head And Neck

Weighed-in, then seated in small squares
arranged to engender...
We share a delay-grumble out loud.
Inside all of us, fear fracks a quake,
but it's curtained with a smile,
or chattered away with a brought-in friend,
until a warm welcome picks on each of us
to move knife-nearer.
My gripped book is never opened,
so many faces to read.

*Up to the nines* for the occasion.
He has his *Telegraph* for grim reading.
They sit together a page-turn apart,
until he folds it to a pocket-stuff;
*in-the-event-of... to be discussed...*
She precision-lists, through crimped lips,
marshalling even flowers in a vase.
He niggles her consenting, notes second signing,
lets some student see what's in her throat.

A chink of handcuffs raises eyes just briefly;
a man is blue-uniformed into a corner.
His half-a-head tumour earns him a knowing nod.

Young heads bowed to their handhold,
whispering their faith in radiation.
I can't see who bears the wound,
then hear her obturator-lisp.
Tear-jerk caught, as we all stare
at the bright through-the-window sky.

Chair bangs, door swings –
an old man's slump is wheeled in.
*Dear, you look so well,* a nurse reassures his ear.
He gums a reply; knows he won't be going home.

## Keeping An Appointment

She totters stick-propped into the reception,
taking someone's steadying hand so that
she can rummage for her card.
Lips tighten to crease an expression,
lip pursing is no longer an option.

Across the years, smiles easily danced between those cheek bones,
but the skin has been stretched with knifed precision, and so
just a taut teething tantamounts a grin.

Computer screen announces it's cancelled.
A hollow *Sorry* echoes in some soft cellar.
Then all the bags and wheels have to be arranged
to allow her body to limp away.

# Why Me?

Her voice was a husk, it crumbled with each rasp,
yet the question she breathed I clearly received.

I wanted to nod it away with a suitable cliché,
but the words didn't stretch, and I couldn't bear
my empty idea floating in air, I could only stare.

I inspected the flowers in the vase,
wincing at each one, they stared back hard.
The question still hung on her tears.

In my jacket-lining I found a lost coin,
palm-squeezed it, maybe its edge would sting a reply,
but it left an empty mark, no answer to why?

Then the visitor's bell rang; everyone to go home.
Of course she had to stay. I never found the answer.
She never asked again.

## Inoperable

She is fighting a bitter blanket war,
bed clothes crumpled in open revolt,
cries for the order she can't restore.
Working hands that once took charge,
tidied piles, tucked in corners, now
hover frail, grip-less; cannot smooth
the creases flat.

Dutiful relatives skirting her bed, just
flickering shadows in the line of her attention,
but she only sees those in her head.

On the high wall before her, a smudge of paint
becomes a mouse engaging in bitter debate,
revealing his envy for the slither of cheese,
lying untouched on the hospital plate.

She smiles at the flowers brought into view,
remarks: *They are beautiful but cut down;*
*vase is a vessel of departure.*

Joyful greetings for unseen visitors;
have they flown through the window,
or descended gracefully from the ceiling?
Though their faces are to us obscure,
her countenance beams at people she knew.

She has something she wants to confide,
so urges them quickly to cross the divide.
Her memories fade incomplete,
as she slips simply into narcotic sleep,
leaving us stranded at the bed side,
wondering whether we've survived.

# Sharing

He lies in the corner, a scant of bone-stretched skin.
Cut to completion, he wants to go home.
Battery dead, he can't hear anything below a shout;
studies mouths to dowse his fears,
catches only: *Love, Dear.*
Sounds like a street proposition, as far as he can recall.
The odd *Mister* would have straightened him up,
like in the days of suits and ties.

Pillows puffed up for doctor's visit;
white coats squared around him.
His options are mouthed, loud for all to hear.
The final sentence hangs in our ears.

## Service User

Her slight frame strains to contain him.
He needs to clutch the banister,
climb the stairs for reasons rubbled in his head.
He aches to continue, but she has a shift to complete.

Her hissed shit, his whimper, form grisly counterpoint.
He must be somehow stashed, coaxing takes time.
On a minimum wage she won't sing a soft sound.

Suddenly big head-nurse arms intercede, and dump him
into a resident's circle to mumble up the past.
He can weep over bits of regret that still flutter,
even in his state of disconnect.

If now a single clear thought could linger long enough,
would it be: I won't bother with tea?

## Left Behind

Tugged from sleep by morning rattle,
a routine of buttons and knots. Dressing-up,
a semblance sufficient to step-out, though
to be invisible would be like warm sunshine.

A tidy house is now just clutter to his
curtained eyes; dust a gentle smother.
A key that didn't turn would be a mercy,
he could ghost the city-maze until his time.

Echoes of the last talk beat in his head;
something fidgeted and straightened.
A breathless slip, the cold thud of nothing more,
except the wish for a faster wither.

There was a ceremony of course; a polite queue,
honed nods, smiles deserving crafted replies, but
words just crossed the street.

Finally a finger buffet; something to tipsy memories,
crumb-spit togetherness, handed-round plates emptied
until all that remained: a dry curl of bread.

## Clearing Out

When she could no longer grip and grope about,
they moved her somewhere clean and clinical,
safe to spill her soup and sing something simple.

Before the curtains are chemically drawn,
a flake of memory carries her home
to dust through each remembered room.

She still hears her bloke's coming and going,
happy feet on the stairs, squeaking springs,
the comfy fill of easy chairs. He died and
took away the best part of her.
The rest just needed shifting out.

The grate is empty and the china cracked,
the table laid with plastic sacks.
It's today they tear her home apart.

Through the door tramp heavy-booted shifters.
Carpets rolled, boards laid bare.
Old newspaper scowls across fifty years.

Dark wood is scuffed across brittle boards,
easy chairs shoulder-high into the bright air,
polished ghosts showing their underwear.

Cupboards gape forgotten wallpaper,
their contents bagged and binned.
She never found a use for that interesting tin.

Out goes her bed, broken into bits,
with its mattress yellow from recent piss.
The only proof she exists: numbered on an auction list.

# Down and Out

# Hot Desking

That used to be his in the corner, now he's just one of five.
Each has a scheduled elbow time; click-on, paper shuffle,
buried in a bag, then out through door bangs.

Chair still slightly angled; years of tensing and slump,
honed for a neighbourly lean, but it always spring-squeaked
him straight when the boss was in sight.

Drawers stuffed with home-from-home; lunch box,
favourite mag, something tacky among the paper-clips.
Locked in the bottom draw, files best forgotten.

Wall in front once pin-holed with – *Wish you were here!*
Now just a list – when his laptop can land.
Needs to look closer – can't see when he is due…

## A Few Words Before Leaving

Time was, he recalled, sipping black scald,
tasks in hand, to be sorted and signed.
Jacketed march to the boss' desk, through
shifting fag smoke and telephone shouts,
darted questions, straightened-back replies,
blame scribbled away, job done, loosened tie.

*It's all scripts and screens today:* he guffawed.
*Not like when I first sat at the desk over there.*
*Was all balanced frowns and double entry talk.*

Yanking open filing drawers in his head,
he edited forty years of corridor chats.
Mates defined in a catch-phrase or two,
Shadow-laughter from the back of the room.

Someone slunk from his crumpled thoughts.
Memory shiver, splash-burnt hand, murmur
of the findings that cut him down, hollowed
the words in his dried-up throat.
Spread of pain to his neck and jaw,
light-headed he slipped to the floor.

No office to cross, he was ergonomically seated,
risk assessed, ready for audit...
*Sit up straight,* his mother used to say,
*it helps you think.*
But uncontrolled, it caused the glitches.

They leant over him briefly to offer support,
but it was all too late, out-placed, logged off.

# Down and Out

Cuts a fine figure from a distance, close up
you see the crumple, the spill of ash.
Bitter winds blew from his stained hand,
the frayed cuffs he forgets to sleeve away.

Once he stormed through swing doors,
his bass-boom gathering secretarial squeals.
Returning wine-soaked, all signed and sealed,
riding roughshod on his high-horse.

Now reception bars his way.
He must sign-in, to be accounted for – in case of fire.
Not used to waiting, time descends to toy with him.
His once smiling lips now just droop.

The meeting hums him to the soft pull of a nap.
Coffee lies cold in a half-drunk cup.
He is referred to in past tense, but waves it away.
Why wrestle with air? Through the window,
he hears the din from the street below.

# On a Point of Leaving

*A second hand furniture shop*

I nursed my purchase, wasn't going to mention more,
but her eyes were full of things to be said. The old bloke gone!

She leant against the furniture stacked up across the years.
Second-hand chairs shaped by a seated generation;
polished up, fabric tacked, might give comfort elsewhere.

*Yes, he died six weeks ago, eighty almost to the day.*
*He was just in the next room*, she said – *echoing out*
*those old stories;* his memories, with a bit of smartening up
could always tickle interest. I miss his cheery pointing-out.

Out like a used bulb, one moment lit, the next
an empty dark, even a long life has its end.
One moment there are things to be said; the next
just stacked wood, and outside a trickle of rain.

## Short-listed

She smiles sincerely at each behind-the-door creak,
wants to be in there, storytelling to match the spec,
pin-striped crumpled and smoothed, then crumpled again,
mouth corners upturned to a fix.

> He taps his iPhone, tunes into heads-ups and sharings,
> reorganising just to stay in his seat.
> Briefcase gripped as if something meaty,
> a snap of locks lays bare an in-flight snack.

She wants to engage him in a crafted chat.
He just nods or murmurs an odd reply. So she decides
to practise eye contact with the ticking clock.

> He becomes book-buried – up to his thought furrows:
> *How to succeed without bothering.*
> Cover display angled in case of glances,
> inside pages jotted with his overdrafts.

Both mouths water at the visual of the corridor coffee-vend.
Who dares to shift in case a call is missed? Nobody comes –
both believe it's a test, so they finger-fiddle time's passage,
until someone does come – to empty the bins.

# Journey's End

He wears his open-neck shirt conforming to dress-down,
sat up straight in his carriage seat, hopes the connection stays alive.
He brushes his keyboard as if a sonata should ensue.
Instead his screen skypes a slump of faces,
voicing *I'm good, thanks* down some tube.
The meeting commences, loudness is mandatory,
confidentiality spread to the nearby.
A battle of bellowing with polite interjections,
his head and neck pumped into a sweaty red-swell.
Something contended is non-negotiable.
He finger knots the live-wire in response to an ultimatum,
and yanks it from its socket. His shirt buttons ping.
In final defiance he yells at them all.
The whole carriage cheers as he falls to the floor.

## The Last Brown Packet

Once you had a box-stacking, air-shouting, and cheery-whistle job,
flat cap mates giving short shrift. Worksheet waving,
pencil behind the ear or the usual fag – you got stuck in,
until a tea urn break, a fold of *The Daily Mirror* to check results.
Dreams pocketed, you were hooted back to lever and stack.

Your life, lockered until the shift end, presentation-clock
to count down the cough-jerked hours, each chime bearing you back
to your bantering mates; old tales packed and delivered into your head.
It was meant to stay steady, but it all stalled.

You were of course stumble-stepped through procedure.
*Yes buts* smiled away, deaf-ears gave undivided attention.
You were told of market forces that beggared belief.
The last brown packet was handed out – *Sorry!* echoed in door-slams.
Loyalty a failed currency – bags of it would buy you a snigger.

Yours is now the Monday walk through stale streets,
email *Hi* to strangers you will never meet.
Best leave your thoughts at home – rights are easily wrecked,
and you are just another coffee stain to wipe away.

# Workaholic

Shuffling his papers in tidy reams
of minutes and memos and follow-up files.
Each piece of paper defines his existence,
seeking perfection with everything written.

He slaves on – outside, darkness descends;
doesn't notice the world has gone home.
Soon life has slipped another day, but he is happy!
All his papers are filed to be found again.

Love and life have escaped his attention;
just subjects to discuss at a future convention.
Perhaps when he delivers his final address:
*I dealt with everything, I did my best.*

All his papers might be tossed in the bin
*Nothing of interest – no time to sin!*
As they carry his coffin, to throw him away:
*His life's work was orderly!* is all they will say.

## Derelict Factory

It was a hall of steam and thunder,
more decibels than any ear should take.
Now a silent shell, stripped to fetch a price,
not even an echo to switch off.
Rusting Excaliburs split the concrete.
Floor pitted with toothless holes once
clutched the steel that bore the shudder.

I see the ghosts of working men in the jokes
they scratched on those grubby walls.
They dreamt to the rhythm of a production run;
scoring hat tricks from their broken stools.
Brown coated foremen ruled their lines,
pitching commands above the machine howl;
bawling out sickies with their bloodshot excuses,
or leaning down on their tossed together teams.

Shifts of strain went through those doors.
All those issues tensing the air; cliques formed, tales told.
If banter had bones, this would be a charnel house.
We went among them with our practised smiles,
sketched a horizon with the future bright.
They whispered: *You can't see that on nights!*
But we were fervent, so they were quiet.
Now litter tumbles across the site.

# Notes on Poems

Stone Silence: *Persilschein*: A colloquial term for a 'clean bill of health', used in post-war Germany to signify that an individual was officially 'denazified' and allowed to re-enter civilian life without restrictions. This process became much faster and easier after 1948 when the US lost interest and shifted focus to their new enemy in the form of the Soviet Union.

Strawberry Girl: *Vopos:* East German policemen, or *'Volkspolizei'*.